In a time whe

literally, when

– Ben Horrex p

...n on to who we are as children of God in Jesus Christ. As we reach for our phones first thing in the morning and post to please an audience of however many, Horrex reminds us that we live to please an audience of One, and that we wake up to a Father who already delights in us, in Christ.

Jerry Taylor, Vicar, Enderby Parish Church, Leicester

Time online is not just a big part of our lives; it's where much of our lives are lived. So it's really important to think through what it means to live the Christian life in an online world. That's what Ben Horrex does in The Gospel Online. *In an accessible and engaging way, Ben shows how the Bible speaks to this issue with relevance and hope.*

Tim Chester, Senior Faculty, Crosslands Training

We live in an age where it is more possible than ever to live a lie. In our identity online, we can so easily inflate our ego, invent multiple personas and hide behind the veil of anonymity. In The Gospel Online, *Ben equips us to navigate this challenging and ever-evolving world, calling us all to live authentically for Jesus online. Here we have a book which I am eager to share with my children, and our young people at church, but also to read and live out myself as we answer the call to live and speak for Jesus online.*

Phil Moore, Musician, Songwriter, Director of Ministry for Cornerstone Church, Nottingham

The Gospel Online *is a great book for helping young people to understand the impact that social media can have on their faith, both in a positive and negative way. It's an engaging read and balances lived experiences and reflections with Scripture and biblical principles. The theology in this book is accessible for young people and it reads like a conversation with a youth worker who really cares about young people. While aimed at young people I also think that it's a brilliant resource for youth leaders and parents to enable them to start conversations about this important subject.*

Mike Kelly, Youth and Families Development Officer, Diocese of Ely

THE GOSPEL
ONLINE

THE GOSPEL ONLINE

WHY THE GOSPEL TRANSFORMS YOUR ONLINE IDENTITY

BEN HORREX

10 Publishing
a division of 10 of those.com

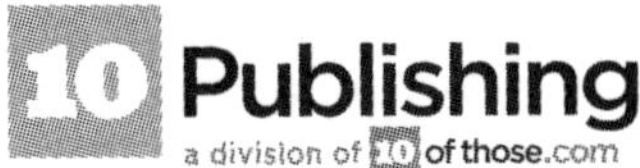

First published in Great Britain in 2022

British Library Cataloguing in Publication Data
A record for this book is available from the British Library

ISBN: 978-1-913896-83-6

Designed by Pete Barnsley (CreativeHoot.com)

Printed in Denmark

10Publishing, a division of 10ofthose.com
Unit C, Tomlinson Road, Leyland, PR25 2DY, England

Email: info@10ofthose.com
Website: www.10ofthose.com

1 3 5 7 10 8 6 4 2

For my wife, Lizzi.
To a life on mission together.

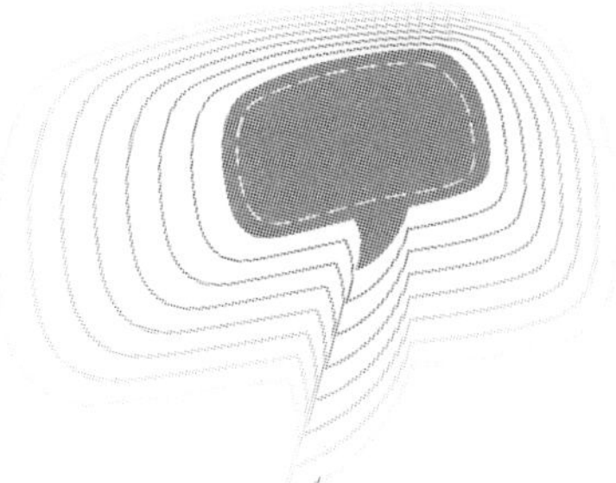

CONTENTS

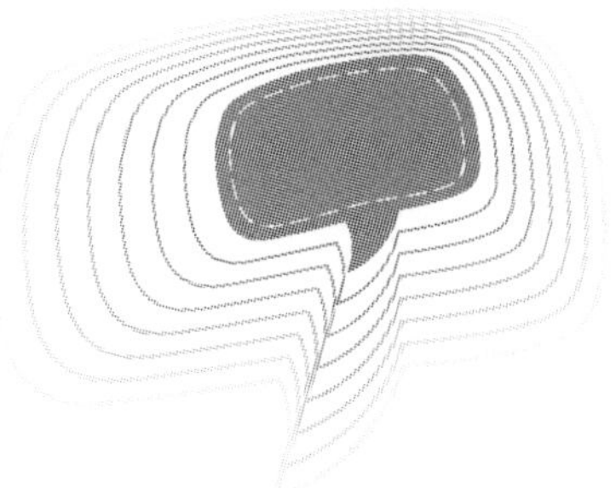

INTRODUCTION

THE PROBLEM WE FACE

I don't know about you, but my time online really matters. There are so many exciting things we can do online, from buying what we want and having it arrive at our doors in a few hours' time to speaking to friends thousands of miles away without having to wait for the post to arrive! We can form genuine friendships and authentic virtual communities, sharing what matters to us.

Maybe you're now able to keep in touch with family far away who you only used to see at Christmas. Maybe you've seen one of your friends go viral with one of their dance videos or streaming on Twitch. Maybe you can't imagine a world where Amazon doesn't deliver what you need tomorrow!

And yet, there are problems with our new online world too. We begin to separate who we are (our person) from who we want others to see (our persona), presenting the best version of ourselves online and hiding the bad bits. Companies boast how great they are, showing off their new recycled cups rather than mentioning the low wages their staff are paid. Individuals shout about how great their recent exam results were rather than how badly they lost their temper with their parents last week.

Social media companies are constantly battling against bullying, hate and extremism, trying to keep their spaces open to free speech while keeping them safe. Plus we waste so much time online! I expect most of those reading this, like me, check their phone within just a few minutes of waking up in the morning and then have it glued to their side. Work is continually interrupted by notifications and family dinners are fighting grounds for whether screens are allowed.

None of these are problems exclusive to social media because we've always had difficulties with things like speech and identity. However, social media tends to accentuate, accelerate and exaggerate the issues we already have. If we had a bad temper before, it's much easier to shoot off a negative comment online than say something face to face. If we're ignoring others in person, the online world is somewhere we can escape easily, consuming and observing rather than interacting. Something we wouldn't say out loud face to face might be something we feel comfortable posting.

As Christians, we should also think through how our faith interacts with our online world. Just because the Bible, a 2000-year-old book, doesn't talk about social media doesn't mean that God is silent on the topic. We need to see the opportunities for evangelism and discipleship online, both sharing our faith and encouraging other Christians in their walk with Jesus.

Maybe you already share the gospel online and show that you're willing to talk with people about your faith. Maybe you share links with friends to videos or websites that can explain a Christian view on issues better than you could in person. Maybe you use your online relationships with other Christians to urge them on in their faith in a kind of unofficial support group. Maybe being online is a good way to spend more time with other members of your church and to celebrate things virtually between seeing each other on Sundays.

We also need to recognise the issues social media presents for Christians. The Bible clearly shows us that our whole lives should revolve around our commitment to God, but our time online can tempt us to focus elsewhere. Adverts pull us towards consumerism. Oversexualised photos and videos tempt us towards unhelpful thoughts and actions. And the growth of advice and 'inspirational' self-help accounts can suggest that answers to our problems should come from the world rather than from God.

Misunderstandings can grow faster online without body language and tone to help, making constructive and sensitive debate difficult. Maybe you thought someone was joking with you online, only realising that they're actually quite hurt by what you said when you see them the next day in school.

Working out what is true in extreme opinions can be exhausting, with fake news and jokes spreading without people knowing that they're not true facts. How we relate to others online can become impersonal. Rather than interacting with others and deepening our relationships, we can become consumed by spending our time looking at advertising, news and clickbait articles. When we do notice that people are struggling in our online communities, it can be overwhelming to know where to start when we have thousands of online relationships.

What we do know is that rules won't fix the problem.[1] No matter how many limits you put on yourself about the amount of time you spend online, the websites you'll visit or the numbers of followers you'll have, the root issue is much bigger.

All of us are sinful people. We 'sin' by rejecting God and how he wants us to live. We have hearts that want to choose and do their own thing in rebellion against God. The truth is if we don't understand how much better God is than all the things that tempt us, sin will control us. Sin transforms us into selfish people, doing things for the wrong reasons and making bad choices,

1 Have a look at Colossians 2:20–23 for why rules can sometimes be unhelpful.

and pulls us away from our God-given identity. We want the never-ending videos and constant scrolling because, in the moment, it can give us more immediate satisfaction than spending time offline. We can forget that we're loved by God and brought into his family because we would rather turn away from him and choose things that give us instant joy, even if they're sometimes not good for us.

And yet, God doesn't abandon us. As Christians, we have 'the gospel', literally the 'good news'. Our gospel is that God came to earth as the person of Jesus to save us. He went to the cross and took all of our sin on himself to save us. He was raised back to life to prove that he had defeated sin and death to save us. The gospel, the good news, is that God loves us and wants us to turn back to him.

Our challenge now is to understand how we can live as those who are loved by God and dependent on him when we're online. We don't want to be people who build up our own identity and forget that we're God's children. We don't want to forget that we're adopted by our heavenly Father, brought into his family and given an amazing new identity as his sons and daughters.

It can be so tempting to inflate and exaggerate our own personality, to feel proud of what we do and who we are. One of my most memorable art projects at primary school was making a paper mache balloon. We blew up a balloon as big as we could before covering it with newspaper dipped in glue. Once it was dry and had hardened, we burst the balloon but the shell survived, ready to be made into something useful like a slightly flimsy bowl or plant pot!

Well, imagine that balloon being blown up more and more is filled with all of our own hype about how good we are and how much we've done for others. When we post about ourselves online, it's then like putting paper mache all over the balloon, so that our great identity seems more solid. Everyone can see how great we are, even when we have days when we feel a bit deflated inside.

The problem is that God doesn't care how good you look on the outside. He doesn't love you because you're the best at sports or get the best grades. He doesn't love you because of that amazing paper mache balloon you're showing off. He loves you even if the balloon inside the paper mache burst long ago and you feel like all that's left is the shell. He loves you because he is gracious and generous. He sees and knows the real you. He loves you even though you are broken and sinful, loving you so much that he sent Jesus to die for you.

As Christians, the power of the gospel will transform every part of our lives. As believers who are trusting in God, we're privileged to have a new identity founded upon what Jesus has done for us. The Bible may not obviously give a perspective on social media on first reading. And yet, God's Word is living and active, showing us principles to live by that will transform our earthly lives. We would be foolish to think that new inventions such as social media aren't included in that transformation.

In the next five chapters, I'm not going to set a series of rules for using our time online or even give you a list of top tips for how to get the most out of social media. Instead, I will trace five significant themes through the Bible. These will show us what it looks like to be a Christian online, living for God's glory and resting in our knowledge that Jesus has saved us – not because of what we do, but because of how gracious God is.

IDENTITY

BEING AUTHENTIC

Have you ever assumed what someone is like based on what you've heard about them, only to meet them and find out that they're completely different? In the past few years, I've met a few people online via Skype or Zoom who I've then discovered are much shorter or taller than I imagined! Webcams can distort things. One colleague I met with online for a whole year turned out to be two metres tall and just had a cleverly positioned webcam. I only realised the truth when I met him in person and had to look up to the sky!

That might be a silly example, but what we share online about ourselves and what we're like can sometimes be really different. Maybe you know someone from school or work who can sometimes be unfair and rude, but who on social media comes across as the nicest person because they're always posting about the good things they do and the people who love them.

Or maybe you know someone who is really shy and quiet, never jumping into conversations unless they're specifically asked. It's then a real surprise if you find that they're constantly tweeting throughout the day, telling the world everything they can – from what they had yesterday for breakfast to their strong views on some very controversial topics.

There are always differences between the person that we are and the persona that we present to others. We want to make ourselves look the best we can. However, social media can exaggerate the difference, giving us a bit of extra distance between who we are in reality and how we want to be seen. We can share what we want, comment when we want and edit anything that doesn't make us look quite right.

While the next chapter will explore how others see us, it's important to first think about how we see ourselves. The good news is that the Bible tells us how to know who we are and live differently, trusting in that new God-given identity.

BIBLICAL PRINCIPLES

Even right at the beginning of the Bible, the first humans – Adam and Eve – began to separate who they were and how they wanted to be seen. They made the decision to turn away from God. As Genesis 3 tells us, they decided that it wasn't enough to be loved by him because they also wanted the power to know what is good and what is evil. They therefore ate the fruit from the tree of knowledge, ignoring God's warning. As Adam and Eve are the representatives of all humans, their disobedience plunged humanity into a new normal of rebellion against God. Having done what they shouldn't, they suddenly saw what they're truly like: naked and vulnerable. They could be seen for who they really were.

Genesis 3 verse 7 says, 'Then the eyes of both of them were opened, and they realised that they were naked; so they sewed fig leaves together and made coverings for themselves.' When they saw that they were exposed, that they were visible to each other and God, they felt the need to cover themselves. They hid themselves from each other and from God.

Adam and Eve hadn't been created with the shame and brokenness that we have now. They were created perfectly, without fault. After God had finished each part of his creation, the Bible tells us clearly, 'God saw that it was good' (Gen. 1:10, 12, 18, 21 and 25). After he had created humans, 'God saw all that he had made, and it was very good' (Gen. 1:31). Humanity was part of the goodness of creation. Initially, they felt no shame being naked and vulnerable around each other and God (Gen. 2:25). And yet, as soon as sin came into the world, Adam and Eve felt the need for clothes to hide something of themselves from each other and their Creator, rather than being vulnerable and revealing themselves (Gen. 3:7).

If we realise that even those first humans tried to show themselves in a better light and hide something of who they were, it's no surprise that we feel the need to hide something of who we are.

Think about the worst thing that you've ever done. Something that you wish you'd never done. Who would you be happy knowing about it? Would you tell your friends, your family, your teachers or your work colleagues?

We have a natural instinct to want to hide our bad things and display our good aspects, splitting the person that people see from the person that we truly are. While it's fine to have some privacy and not to want everyone in the world to see every bit of our lives, we tend to try and polish up our identity to make ourselves look a bit better. And if we're not careful, our identity becomes more connected to the persona we've constructed, the polished version of ourselves, than the honest assessment and knowledge of who we are to God.

The Bible is very clear that while we might manage to hide from others, there's no way to hide from God. In the Garden of Eden, Adam and Eve couldn't hide their sin from him.

Paul, one of the most famous Christians in history, became a believer soon after Jesus' death and resurrection, going on to set up many churches. Many of his letters to those congregations are in the Bible, showing us what it looks like to live as Christians. In 1 Corinthians 4:3–5, part of his letter to the church in Corinth, we read:

> *I care very little if I am judged by you or by any human court; indeed, I do not even judge myself. My conscience is clear, but that does not make me innocent. It is the Lord who judges me. Therefore judge nothing before the appointed time; wait until the Lord comes. He will bring to light what is hidden in darkness and will expose the motives of the heart. At that time each will receive their praise from God.*

There's no hiding from God because he sees all. He brings light to the darkness, exposing everything that we are, both the good and bad. Every time you've cringed and wished someone couldn't see what you've done and couldn't know what runs through your mind, God sees and knows. His is the opinion that matters because he is the one who knows us completely, who can 'expose the motives of the heart', seeing not just what we've done but why we've done it.

God looks into our hearts and sees how broken we are. Nothing is hidden from his sight.[2] He sees that we continually want to be selfish,

---

2 For more on the power of God's Word, the Bible, to get to the truth of what we're like, take a look at Hebrews 4:12–13.

to make life easier for ourselves at the expense of others, to take more than we deserve, to bend the truth to make ourselves look good. He sees you, not the polished-up persona you hide behind.

If someone could see that level of depth – every thought you had, every action you took – and knew why you did those things, what would their reaction be? If someone knew me, my thoughts and my actions – without my persona showing off only my good qualities – they would definitely see me very differently.

And yet, God reacts in a way that we might not expect. While we might feel shame, God is a relational God who reaches out to us.

God sees who you are, every bit of you, and still loves you. He loves you so much that he sent his Son Jesus to the cross to rescue you. He didn't do that because of the persona you present or the good works you manage. He saved you for the person you are – someone who is broken and sinful, but seeking a Saviour and looking for hope in him.

In another of his letters to churches, Paul wrote this: '… for all have sinned and fall short of the glory of God, and all are justified freely by his grace through the redemption that came by Christ Jesus' (Rom. 3:23–24).

None of us is good enough to come before our amazing, perfect, all-powerful God as we are. We fall short, we make mistakes, we fail. And yet, Jesus went to the cross to redeem us, to pay for everything bad we've ever done or said or thought. Every bit of that broken person that you want to hide away from others is redeemed, fixed, perfected by God because of the great sacrifice Jesus made.

Later in the same letter Paul reiterates, 'But God demonstrates his own love for us in this: while we were still sinners, Christ died for us' (Rom. 5:8).

God doesn't love you because you've fixed your image and made yourself look perfect to the world. God doesn't only love the façade you put up for others to see. God doesn't love your perfect church personality on a Sunday more than your everyday reality at school or work.

God showed that he loved us, his broken and sinful people, when Jesus went to the cross for us. Jesus died not because of the good things that we've done but so that we might experience the goodness of God's love.

Therefore, we have no reason to put up a façade for God, even if it feels like we should sometimes. He knows you inside out and loves you because, if you trust in Jesus and ask God for forgiveness of all you've done wrong, you've been washed clean and made perfect. While all Christians will still mess up sometimes, there's something very different about us. As followers of Jesus, our identity has changed.

Think about how you introduce yourself to someone new. Often, after giving your name, you might tell them how old you are, where you live or grew up, what you do for a job or which school you go to. They're the sort of things that we find helpful to understand who a person is and how we can relate to them.

While the Bible doesn't tell us to avoid these being part of who we are, they aren't the core of our identity. Further on in Paul's letter he explains:

> *For those who are led by the Spirit of God are the children of God. The Spirit you received does not make you slaves, so that you live in fear again; rather, the Spirit you received brought about your adoption to sonship. And*

> *by him we cry, 'Abba, Father.' The Spirit himself testifies with our spirit that we are God's children (Rom. 8:14–16).*

Our core identity, the thing that we build everything else upon, is that we're God's children. That's our new identity when we trust in Jesus. So, we don't need to be fearful of how people will see us. Nor do we need to stay enslaved by the idea that we must always do more and be better.

If we have asked for forgiveness from God and committed ourselves to him, we have God's Spirit living in us who helps us to live with that changed identity. He encourages us to call out to God as Father when we're in trouble because we are his children.

No longer will we need to show off and try to polish up our appearance. It doesn't matter whether you've been born into a rich or poor family, whether you've gone to church since you were a baby or whether you've only recently heard about Jesus. It doesn't even matter how many followers you have to show off to virtually!

We're children of God because of what Jesus has done, giving us forgiveness by his grace.

That's the foundation that everything else must be based upon.

That doesn't mean that everything else in your life needs to be thrown out. You don't need to give up your membership of your local football team, abandon your family or hide which town you were born in. However, it does mean that you need to see every bit of your identity as secondary compared to your identity as a child of God. No matter how important other aspects of your life feel, they must be seen through the lens of your identity in Christ.

Think about what the world would look like if you put on glasses with coloured lenses. If they were pink lenses, everything would look pink. If they were blue, everything would look blue. The things that you see are still there, but they change appearance because of the lens you're looking through.

Being a child of God doesn't mean that there can't be other aspects to your identity, but it does mean that you need to look at those things in a different light. The place you were born, the friends you have or the type of person you see yourself as now need to be seen through the lens of being a child of God. The identity that we've been given by God – the knowledge that we're loved by him, created by him, saved by him – must be the only thing that shapes the core of our identity. Nothing else can ever come above that identity. Anything else we construct and add needs to be secondary to the identity we receive from God.

That identity is completely secure and will never be broken, though you may change other parts of your identity. If you accept God as your King and Saviour, you will never lose your identity as God's child in all your life. You will forever be one who is forgiven by the Creator of this world, loved because of what Jesus did for you and destined to be with him in heaven for eternity. That's an identity worth clinging to.

THE DANGER

Forgetting your identity

How you see yourself is fundamental, but there are two main dangers in the area of identity: forgetting your primary identity or letting your secondary identities become primary.

Firstly, can you remember a time when your faith, while valuable, didn't seem as important as it should? A time when you had quite a low view of your faith? For those who've grown up in the church, there's a time when you have to decide: Do I trust in Jesus? Is this real? Am I willing to live differently? Am I willing to show that I'm a Christian online?

Without asking those questions, we can fall into a pattern of generally calling ourselves a 'Christian' without thinking it's that important. It can be nice to sometimes go to church on a Sunday, but family and friends can seem more important than Jesus. Time at football practice, dance rehearsal and on the Xbox might feel just as good as church. Prayer is a nice concept and might help us to talk through our problems, but just getting on with doing something seems a better use of time than voicing it to God.

The problem here is that this isn't just a case of a Christian struggling a little or not being confident to talk about God online. This is a case of forgetting who they are!

If Jesus is God, the one who created the world and the one who went to the cross to die for you, being a follower of him is what defines who you are! His love, his grace, his sacrifice is something that can't be ignored.

That's why we want to prioritise being at church, reading the Bible, spending time in prayer with God and getting to know other Christians. Not because those things make us better Christians and help us to earn God's love, but because those things continually bring us back to the truth: we're God's children and that matters more than anything else.

So, when you spend time online, be on the lookout for things that drag your identity away from knowing you are a child of God. Be on the lookout for when your online presence is missing any reference to God, when your Instagram profile could be the profile of anyone, regardless of their trust in Jesus. If no one would have a clue that you're a Christian unless they asked you directly or caught you walking out of the church door, maybe change is needed!

Secondly, while someone might have a really high view of their relationship with God, a common danger is that they have an even higher view of one of their secondary identities.

While we might love being a great sibling, striving to be a good friend, growing as a football player or dreaming of being a nurse in the future, those identities should never be more important than your God-given identity as his child. Our relationship with him shapes everything we do. That's the most fundamental thing about us.

The danger is that sometimes our friends can look at us online and it's much clearer that we're passionate about our hobbies, sports teams and relationships than our identity as a Christian. The videos, pictures and comments we share about God can be much less frequent than how much we share about our holidays, our rugby team's latest win or the meal we had last night.

It's definitely not a bad thing to love the sport that you're good at, to get excited about the sequel to your favourite programme or to love spending lots of time with your family. The problem is when you love those things so much that they define who you are more than your relationship with God. When your time with God is less important than your time with your teammates. When you're willing to compromise what you believe God tells you in the Bible because it doesn't sit well with what your friends think. How many of your interactions online would change if you no longer believed in Jesus?

As we saw earlier, God created lots of good things and he wants us to enjoy them and to love them. But when we start to love the things God has created more than the Creator himself, we've made a big mistake. If you get a present from someone who is really important to you, it would be a bit odd if you loved the present more than you love the person!

Imagine if, this Christmas, your parents give you an expensive and thoughtful gift that you'd been asking for repeatedly throughout the year. You open the gift, almost in disbelief that they've bought it for you. And yet, when they ask you if you like it, you just ignore them. You decide that you never need to speak to them again because they've given you the gift you wanted. You don't need them anymore!

Doesn't that sound wrong? Surely, the relationship you have with them is more important than the things they've given you to enjoy. And yet that's often what we do with God. We love the things he gives us more than we love our relationship with him.

Don't let a secondary identity become your primary identity. God's love is transformative and nothing else can match it. Being good at golf is nothing like being a follower of the Creator of the universe. Being one of three siblings isn't as important as being a child of God.

These good gifts aren't better than the identity God has given you of being in relationship with him. So, make sure that your online connections and communities never become the most important part of your life.

THE GOAL

A new primary identity

We've established that the most important part of our identity is that we're God's children; nothing else comes close to that. That means that while secondary things aren't unimportant, we need to make that primary identity much more important.

Most of all, it means prioritising time where we can foster our new identity. If we're God's children, we can spend time talking with him in prayer, prioritise time listening to him in his Word (the Bible) and make the most of the time worshipping alongside others who are saved by Jesus too. The Holy Spirit, who has lived in us ever since we trusted in God to save us, energises us to live like this.

Truly seeing ourselves primarily as children of God will be really difficult if the time we give to God is, at best, minimal. Put aside the first ten minutes in the morning that you'd normally spend scrolling through TikTok and use them to open the Bible and hear from God. Download a good prayer app or Bible reading plan. Foster your God-given identity and you'll find yourself seeing much more clearly how the other parts of your identity can work with and not against your faith. Your online presence can then begin to more authentically reflect who you are.

Your primary identity will give you life and free you up to do more, rather than restricting you to things you don't enjoy. It might sound obvious, but God doesn't make your life worse; he makes it much better! He wants to make your online world even better, with a rock-solid foundation built upon his love for you.

It's almost like God's given you a script to show you the best way to live as this new person – as his child. Being loved by God and having the security of being his child is like being giving the starring role in the best production, with a part like no other. He shows us in the Bible what it looks like to have him as Father, to live for him, to speak for him. That script doesn't control us; it frees us from forever looking for our identity and desperately searching for meaning.

Alongside fostering that identity, make sure that your identity isn't hidden from those around you. When you introduce yourself, what do you first tell people? For many, saying that you're a Christian is quite a big step and feels almost embarrassing. But if you truly believe that Jesus is your Saviour who has saved you from death and given you a life worth living, surely living authentically means living out your God-given identity?

Don't just tell people about Jesus because 'you should', but because it's who you are. If you're God's child and experience his amazing love for you, expect that to flow out of you to those around you, changing what you say and do.

The reality is that most people won't think you're that odd for talking about Jesus. A post about church on your profile won't end the world! Most conversations I have about my faith are brief and uneventful, and I don't expect that every person I talk to about Jesus will want to immediately read the Bible with me! But that doesn't mean that those conversations aren't really valuable. They show who I am and what I think is important, making belief in God more relatable and opening the door for further questions.

Why not do your best to show that your primary identity is as a child of God? That this is clearly more important than the work you do, the place you live or the hobbies you enjoy?

In fact, showing your primary identity of faith in Jesus online could actually be easier than speaking to someone in person. There are opportunities for posting a Bible verse that really struck you in the sermon at church, posting a picture of the game you played at the church youth club or celebrating when one of your friends gets baptised. All of these are small steps towards being more open about your faith.

Look at the bio you have on Instagram, TikTok or whichever site you use most. Does it talk about who you are? Does God get a mention?

The goal isn't to force the gospel down the throat of everyone you meet, but to live as a child of God and make sure that identity is visible to others. First and foremost, you're defined by your relationship with God and his love for you, and we want to make that clear to others.

If someone looked at you and saw that there's something different about you, wouldn't it be brilliant if they knew why?

QUESTIONS TO THINK ABOUT

1. What is part of your online identity?
2. Which things you listed from question 1 are positive and which are negative? Why?
3. Which of your answers to question 1 sometimes come above God or between you and God?
4. Where might you need a lesser view of your secondary identity?
5. Where might you need a higher view of your God-given, primary identity?
6. What is one step you could take this week to cling to your God-given identity more tightly online?

NAME

REPUTATION MATTERS

If you were asked to think of someone with a huge reputation and a famous name, who would come to mind? Maybe a top footballer, a popular influencer, a TV personality or a big brand. They most likely spend time crafting the images and videos they post online, adding filters for the best light and thoroughly planning the captions they write to engage people well. Sometimes they get caught out when their edits become dishonest and we notice. We call out the weight loss adverts that clearly use edited photos to make models look better, and we protest when brands try to put a positive spin on something they've done wrong.

The reality, though, is that we all like to improve our standing. We often spend time making sure that our reputation among friends, family and complete strangers is as good as it can be. The first few videos on your TikTok profile or the photos you've edited for your Instagram can say a lot about who you are and how you want to be seen. Social media has the potential to really shape who we are online.

I know that's how I felt when I was a teenager. Updating your profiles with photos, pages you liked and who you were friends with was a really big thing. It was a huge deal if you blocked someone and they couldn't see what you were posting anymore. Your likes showed whether you were a fan of the local football team or the big-name club. Or whether you liked the TV show that everyone was talking about or preferred shows that no one else had heard of.

The biggest update possible was changing your relationship status. My friends would regularly and suddenly flick from being 'in a relationship' to 'it's complicated'. What did that mean? And why did I need to know?! Relationships were no longer private or just the topic of whispered gossip. Instead, photos appeared of couples together, and their likes of each other's posts were seen by the world.

Social media is life's billboard to give a flavour of who you are. It's a window into your life over which you have some control. Living our lives online can be an opportunity to reinvent ourselves – or at least to polish up the edges of our appearance and character. To give some more shine to the areas that are a bit grubby. To hide the things that we don't want anyone to see. We can establish a new reputation, especially with the people that we only know online rather than seeing every day at school or work.

And that feels important when so much of how we live our lives revolves around others' opinion of us. Their view of us matters. The most important voice to you might be your friends or your family, or maybe it's someone else.

Social media gives us the chance to make a name for ourselves on our own terms by only displaying the best of our life. Our reputation becomes more and more linked to how we're seen online by others, and less and less linked to the name and reputation we can have in Jesus. But where does the Bible say we should base our reputation?

BIBLICAL PRINCIPLES

Our name and reputation isn't a missing theme from the pages of the Bible. Genesis 11 is perhaps the most famous example of what it looks like to try to make a name for yourself away from God.

After God had punished Adam and Eve for rejecting his authority, sin still stuck around. People had become so wicked that God wiped out everyone by a flood, except Noah and his family, who took refuge on an ark. Even after that, though, sin was still a major problem.[3] By Genesis 11, all the people, who shared one language, were working together to build a huge tower. The problem was not that they wanted to construct a tower, but why they wanted to build it. Verse 4 reads:

> *Then they said, 'Come, let us build ourselves a city, with a tower that reaches to the heavens, so that we may make a name for ourselves; otherwise we will be scattered over the face of the whole earth.'*

---

3 To read more about what the world was like before this story, see the opening ten chapters of Genesis.

As humanity continued to wander away from God and towards sin, the people focused on their own reputation and that of their city. They longed to climb towards the heavens, creating something so majestic that they would be known for what they'd done. Known for how great they were.

But God intervened in order to stop them. He confused the people's language so that they couldn't work together. God scattered them across the world so that they could no longer build the tower that would make a name for themselves. He prevented the foundation of their lives being the greatness they made for themselves, rather than their reputation as God's children.

Their sin was so serious that their Creator God stepped in to stop their creation of the tower. God didn't want them to be known as self-made rebels. He wanted them to know him and know that they were his children. He wanted all of their actions to point towards him, not themselves.

God created people so that he could share his love with them. They were created to worship him alone, not to seek the worship of others because of what they could do. Their reputation and name mattered.

This is often so true of us. When we're online, we hunger for a good name. We can want the prestige of being well-liked, of being popular and of attracting likes on our latest posts. We can search for security, controlling how people see us. We can try to build up followers and likes to make us feel valued. We can feel embarrassed about how people see us in the physical world and look online for a new name, a better reputation. Many of us fall into that Babel mindset.

It's so different to the way that God blessed Abram, soon to be Abraham, in just the next chapter (Genesis 12). God called on Abram – an unknown figure at this point in Genesis – to leave his home and set out for a new, unknown home. Through this, God would bless him. Through this, Abram would start a remarkable journey which would display God's faithfulness. Verses 2 and 3 say:

I will make you into a great nation,
and I will bless you;
I will make your name great,
and you will be a blessing.

I will bless those who bless you,
and whoever curses you I will curse;
and all peoples on earth
will be blessed through you.

God was pouring out his blessing upon Abram. Abram's name would be made great – not through Abram's marvellous acts or through his own ability, but through a covenant, a promise, made with God. It was Abram's dependence on the Creator God, his God – rather than on the things he did – that gave Abram a great name.

In this, we see a clear difference between what is good and bad, between what is godly and sinful, when forming a reputation. When the people planned their construction of the Tower of Babel, they sought to make their name great through the work of their hands. As they stretched towards the heavens, they rebelled against God. They tried to achieve greatness, fight for glory and establish themselves, forgetting the reputation God had given them. He gave them their name and he called them his people, based not on their own work but on their relationship to him.

Abram – a descendent of Noah – didn't deserve the privilege of being the father of a great nation because of who he was. He was given land, he was to become the father of many and his name was made great because of God's blessing on him. Abram then trusted in God's plan, left his home and followed God's direction, and so God transformed Abram's life.

Abram made a good number of mistakes that we read about in the book of Genesis. For example, Abram lied not once but twice about his wife, pretending she was instead his sister, because he was worried that his enemies might kill him and take his wife for their own.[4] And yet, even with all his mistakes and times of failing to trust God, Abram is remembered for being a man of God. He was saved by his faith in God rather than his own works (Heb. 11:17–19).

Another great man of the Old Testament, David, heard a similar promise in 2 Samuel 7. David's life too showed significant sin. He regularly had to come before God to apologise, turning away from all that he did wrong. And

---

4 You can read about these two incidents in Genesis 12:10–20 and Genesis 20.

yet, God poured out his blessing on David, this broken man. As God's chosen king, David was blessed with wealth, power and status. He was blessed with a promise that his house would be established forever (vv. 11–16). In other words, his children would forever be on the throne. This eventually led to David's distant descendant Jesus becoming our eternal King. It's one of the highest blessings that God could bestow on anyone.

God's blessing included something else too. God promised David that his name would be made great:

> *I have been with you wherever you have gone, and I have cut off all your enemies from before you. Now I will make your name great, like the names of the greatest men on earth (v. 9).*

As with Abraham, it was not the greatness of the man that made his name known. The choice and blessing of God is what makes your name known. David was the youngest son in his family, having been almost overlooked in the search for a king until God intervened in 1 Samuel 16. David was not anointed as king because of his strength, wisdom, power or wealth. He was anointed because he was the one chosen by God to be made great.

When we look at David's life, we see a man who was dependent on God. Even in his failures, when he sinned and made foolish choices, he trusted in God. He knew that he was given his kingdom and his reputation by God. Here was a man who didn't deserve the blessing God gave, but was chosen by God.

Many of the psalms in the Bible were written by David. They show his trust in God, his frequent returns to repentance after sin and his thankfulness for the blessings he received. David knew his name was made great by God's blessing, not through the work of his own hands.

Each of these examples shows us just a little of what it looks like to be blessed when trusting in God for reputation. Blessing comes from having faith in our Creator God, not from boasting in our own talents. It's a challenge to our desire to build our online reputation based on our own merit and good works. It's a call to trust that our reputation as a child of God is enough.

And yet, Jesus is our ultimate example of having a name blessed by God. He trusted in God completely and perfectly, from his birth in a humble manger all the way to his death on the cross. He chose to walk towards his death, knowing that his Father's plan was good and was needed for the sake of all humankind. Despite knowing what lay ahead for him, he didn't run away from God's salvation plan. He prayed, 'Father, glorify your name!' (John 12:28). He went to the cross so that his Father's name would be glorified, made great, honoured.

Jesus had more trust in his Father than anyone, including Abraham and David. He never wavered and never sinned. He followed his Father's will, even when that meant sacrificing his own life.

Jesus could have built up his reputation, doing more miracles, healing more people and telling them to spread the word about him. Instead, Jesus actually kept his work quiet at times, telling those he healed or saved not to tell others about him.[5] He wanted people to look to God

---

5 For some examples of this, see Matthew 8:4; 12:16; 16:20; 17:9; Mark 1:44; 3:12; 7:36; 8:30; 9:9; Luke 5:14; 8:56; 9:21, 36.

(Mark 5:19) rather than make his own name and actions great in and of themselves.

But God did make Jesus' name great. He gave him the greatest reputation – 'the name that is above every name' (Phil. 2:9). Jesus, God's Son, was both fully God and fully man. He was the only person in history to be completely obedient to God. The only one who was not stained with sin. The only one whose name and reputation is perfect.

And God gave Jesus many great names. At his birth, the angel told Joseph to name him Jesus because he would be the one who 'will save his people from their sins' (Matt. 1:21). He was also to be called Immanuel as he was 'God with us' (Matt. 1:23), the one who came to humanity and walked alongside us. In the book of Hebrews, he is called the 'great high priest' (Heb. 4:14), who could empathise with us, understand our weaknesses and speak on our behalf to God the Father.

The names Jesus was given show who he was and point to the God who saves his people.

Being sinless didn't mean that Jesus was never tempted to step away from his trust in God and instead build his name and reputation independently. Jesus was tempted by the devil to make a name for himself without God. The devil said that Jesus would be given authority over the whole earth if he bowed down to the devil. But instead of choosing to walk away from his Father, Jesus reiterated his commitment to worship God alone (Matt. 4:8–10). He knew that nothing matched the reputation given to those who trust in God and worship him alone.

Jesus is blessed with the greatest reputation because of his dependence on the Father. Because he trusted wholeheartedly in the goodness of God. Because he could do nothing without the Father (John 5:19).

When we think through what it looks like to have a reputation and name while honouring God, we must look to the biblical examples of David and Abraham, and ultimately to Jesus. He trusted wholeheartedly in his heavenly Father and was blessed with a name and reputation that will never fade.

Jesus is also the only name we will ever need because no other name can save us (Acts 4:12). Let us trust in him and his reputation above all else when considering how others see us.

THE DANGER

The need for approval

Are there times when you fall into the temptation of being like those people building the Tower of Babel? Is building your own reputation through your personality, your work and your image the most important thing to you? Does it feel particularly good when someone knows your name because of what you've done and who you are?

This desire to find approval and impress others shows the condition of our heart. We're no longer content with the approval of our heavenly Father when we instead search for the approval of those around us. Scraping around for positive comments, more likes and signs of approval, to improve our reputation or make our name known, is a problem.

The immediate satisfaction we get from the likes and retweets feels good. A pat on the back or being mentioned by name because of what we did, how we look or our talents can lift us. And yet, that foundation is unstable when the praise ends and the criticism starts. That foundation will never truly satisfy, even if the praise continues throughout our lives.

It's not necessarily sinful to have built a reputation for yourself. The problem is when your motivation for making your name known is to highlight your own greatness rather than God's.

God makes us perfect through the sacrifice of Jesus and promises to be with us for eternity. No amount of polishing is needed to come before God. We're accepted because of the work of his Son at the cross when he died for us and rose again, defeating sin so that we could be with God.

Social media may not create this problem, but it can exaggerate it. While bragging about yourself can feel a bit awkward in person, online it can be much easier to post about your latest achievement. It's simpler to upload the photos that show you in the best light and not to post the embarrassing moments. And so you can put the spotlight on your own gifts and achievements, rather than trying to point to God's glory even in your weakness.

Don't slip into the danger of searching for approval by continually reshaping yourself online. Don't hope that, one day, those around you will see you for who you truly are and that will be enough. God sees who you truly are right now: a broken sinner; someone who can't save themselves. And yet, if you've given your life to Jesus, your name has been made great before God because of what Jesus has done for you at the cross. Trust in him. Rest in his salvation and grace to make your name known. That reputation is priceless.

THE GOAL

Resting in and pointing to God's reputation and grace

What does it look like for you to rest in God's name and his plan for you? To want a reputation that comes from God, rather than boasting about your achievements and gifts above all? It's not wrong to use our gifts and good qualities, or even for people to know that we have them. However, we can use them to serve God, to point to him and to build his kingdom on this earth by telling people about him.

Abraham trusted in God, moving away from his comfortable life in order to pursue what was better. He is remembered for his faith in the promises of God and was given the amazing blessings of land, a great name and many descendants. David trusted in God, even when others overlooked him in their search for a king and even when he faced danger. His faith was seen by God and he was blessed with a great name, with his descendants on the throne forever through Jesus.

Jesus is our perfect example of what it looks like to trust in God alone for our reputation and name. He was given names that showed his relationship to God. His obedience pointed to the goodness and graciousness of the Father. Even the things that made him look great, like his power to perform miracles, revealed more of the plan of God.

What does it look like for you to trust that your faith is what makes a name for you? To know that God blesses you through his grace and so not to strive on your own to gain a reputation? For your social media to show something of your reliance on God for your reputation?

When you trust in God, in his grace and mercy, you'll be transformed. Instead of desiring greatness based on your own merit and good works, you'll be trusting in the Bible's wonderful assurances that we are loved by God and will be with him in eternity. The one who matters most knows us by name because of his Son's sacrifice for us. That's far better!

Earlier, we saw some reasons why we might desire a great name and a great reputation. And yet, God gives us everything we need. He gives us significance, security and the prestige of inheriting eternal life with the Creator of our existence.

We're not promised riches and fame in this life, or that our names will be made great to those around us, but we're promised that our name will be known by the only one who truly matters. As we work in this world, living out our faith online, let's pray that we point people to God's glory and not our own. Rather than showing off our skills and gifts, they should give us more reason to praise the great God who gave us those talents. By forgiving others, serving others and loving them well, people will look at what they see of us online and see someone who is dependent on God.

Let our lives be built on the foundation of who God is and his love for us – as shown to us in the Bible and in the person of Jesus – so that it's his name and reputation that spreads. And let us, like Jesus in John 12:28, strive to glorify God in all we do.

QUESTIONS TO THINK ABOUT

1. Look at the social media account that you use most. Do you think it points towards your glory or to God's?
2. Are there areas of your life where you feel the temptation to 'make your name known'? Why do you find that tempting?
3. How do we glorify God in our social media presence rather than glorifying ourselves?
4. Do you think it's possible to be a Christian influencer? What might be the challenges? What might be the opportunities?
5. What is one step you could take this week to point to God's name rather than your own?

WORD

USING OUR SPEECH

Words are incredibly powerful. If you're a member of any online groups on platforms like Facebook, Discord, Twitter or Reddit, it's pretty clear that things can get heated very quickly. An innocent-looking post about a new game that's just come out can explode into an argument about which new console is the only one a sensible person would choose! Discussion about abstract topics becomes personal and insults are thrown, with those who comment often quite unknown by the people they're arguing with.

Have you ever been made fun of or felt attacked by someone's words? What did it feel like?

It can hurt when someone's speech is used to pull you down rather than build you up. As with many of the things we've already talked about, that's not a problem exclusive to social media. But being hidden away behind a screen can make it so much easier to say things we might feel were unacceptable in person.

At the other end of the spectrum, have you ever been encouraged and built up by someone's words? What did it feel like?

We like to be encouraged by someone else, built up by their kind words and spurred on by their validation. A thoughtful comment on photos, a well-meaning message or a post from a proud parent can improve our mood hugely.

The Bible tells us that while we should never depend on the words of others to give us identity (which, as we saw in chapter one, is given to us by God), we should recognise the power that our words have. The words we use online can have a greater reach and last much longer than those said face to face. If done well, it's possible to use our words biblically and positively. We should take seriously the damage that hurtful words can cause and highly value the power of words of encouragement, both to those who follow Jesus and those who don't.

BIBLICAL PRINCIPLES

God's words are incomparably powerful. In the opening chapter of the Bible, we hear what he can do by his speech. Genesis 1 repeats the phrases 'And God said … And it was so'. The way he created everything that is in existence, bringing about all that we know, was through his word.

We, as humans, are not God. And yet, we also know that we are created to be something like God. In Genesis 1:27, we're told:

> *So God created mankind in his own image,*
> *in the image of God he created them;*
> *male and female he created them.*

We're created in the image of God, made to reflect something of who he is and what he is like. If God's words are powerful, creating the world, it suggests that our words will also be powerful. While we can't use our words to bring things into being in the same way as our Creator God, we should expect our words to have power.

The problem is that since the beginning of time, humans have not used their powerful words solely for good purposes. In Genesis 3, when Adam and Eve first sinned (the Fall), words were centre stage in their rebellion against God. First the snake twisted God's words. Eve twisted them further. Then the snake questioned the goodness of God by tempting humanity to sin (Gen. 3:1–4). And rather than come clean about their actions, Adam and Eve chose to lie to God about what they had done. Adam and Eve chose to use their words poorly and brought upon humanity the curse of sin. We desire to use our words for selfish means. The improper use of our words is a thread that runs a long way back.

For believers today, we have plenty of teaching as to how our words should be used, especially in the Old Testament. Glen Scrivener notes this 'life' and 'death' language is a theme in the book of Proverbs, with words used powerfully, either for good or evil.[6]

---

6 For more information on this and to see the references used in the next paragraph in more detail, take a look at this all-age talk written by Glen Scrivener: https://christthetruth.net/2010/08/26/words-in-proverbs-all-age-sermon/ (accessed 28 September 2021).

Used poorly, our words can be like a 'scorching fire' (Prov. 16:27), 'swords' (Prov. 12:18), 'arrows of death' (Prov. 26:18) and a weight that 'crushes the spirit' (Prov. 15:4). Compare this to the way that words can build us up. They are described as being like food that can 'nourish many' (Prov. 10:21), providing 'healing' (Prov. 12:18) and acting as a 'tree of life' (Prov. 15:4).

Our speech to others matters. When we repeatedly use our words unhelpfully, this causes conflict, arguments and hurt. In contrast, the words we use to build others up can bring life and nourishment to those we know. We should understand the power that our words have and our responsibility to use them well.

If that teaching wasn't conclusive enough, we also have a perfect example of how we should use our words. When we want to distinguish what is life-giving and what is destructive, we can look to Jesus. In him, we see how to control our tongue and use our words to build others up, glorifying God in what we say.

For example, Jesus shows us the right way to use our words when we're frustrated or angry. We might think that getting frustrated or angry is always sinful, but that isn't true. Jesus, the one who did nothing wrong, shows us how to be angry in the correct way. In Mark 11:15–17, we see an example of Jesus' righteous anger, when strong words were needed:

> *On reaching Jerusalem, Jesus entered the temple courts and began driving out those who were buying and selling there. He overturned the tables of the money-changers and the benches of those selling doves, and would not allow anyone to carry merchandise through the temple courts. And as he taught them, he said, 'Is it not written: "My house will be called a house of prayer for all nations"? But you have made it "a den of robbers".'*

The way that the temple was being used was completely wrong. The place meant for worship and prayer was being used as a marketplace. A place for profit rather than prayer. Jesus drove out those who did wrong, overturning the tables of the sellers and criticising them for using 'a house of prayer' as 'a den of robbers'.

Clearly, it's not wrong to use strong words, even in anger, if those words are justified and right. Jesus' words were based on Scripture and were spoken to achieve a righteous outcome, ensuring that the temple was used for God-honouring purposes.

The problem we have is that the majority of our frustrated and angry words aren't used to accomplish righteous things. They're used to hurt others, they're careless or they're full of grumbling and complaining, especially against God. When we use negative language, or get frustrated or angry, we must check our motivations and our language. Are we seeking to call out what is wrong for the right reasons? Or are we just trying to make ourselves look good and prove that we're right?

We might forget that our words have a lot of power. We might think that very little of what we say is taken to heart. But if we're honest, we know that what others say to us can really change how we feel.

Writing to Christians, James speaks of the power of the tongue:

> *When we put bits into the mouths of horses to make them obey us, we can turn the whole animal. Or take ships as an example. Although*

> *they are so large and are driven by strong winds, they are steered by a very small rudder wherever the pilot wants to go. Likewise, the tongue is a small part of the body, but it makes great boasts. Consider what a great forest is set on fire by a small spark. The tongue also is a fire, a world of evil among the parts of the body. It corrupts the whole body, sets the whole course of one's life on fire, and is itself set on fire by hell (James 3:3–6).*

We mustn't underestimate the power of what we say. James uses the examples of important and powerful things controlled by something quite small. A large animal like a horse is controlled by a rider using just a small bit in its mouth. A huge ship is controlled by a captain using just a small rudder. A terrible forest fire can be started by just a small spark.

Even though we might think that our words aren't important unless they're especially positive or negative, what we say can have a devastating effect if it's hurtful. James continues:

> *With the tongue we praise our Lord and Father, and with it we curse human beings,*

> *who have been made in God's likeness. Out of the same mouth come praise and cursing. My brothers and sisters, this should not be. Can both fresh water and salt water flow from the same spring? My brothers and sisters, can a fig-tree bear olives, or a grapevine bear figs? Neither can a salt spring produce fresh water (James 3:9–12).*

As the tongue has huge power, what we say, whether it's 'praise' or 'cursing', will have an effect. When we're online and interacting with someone, it can be tempting to say things that we know are unhelpful, maybe even using stronger words than we would if we could see the reaction of the person in front of us.

Nor are the words we use just important in and of themselves. They also show something of who we are. James asks, 'can a fig-tree bear olives, or a grapevine bear figs?' The answer is obviously no! A tree can't bear the fruit of another tree.

So it is with us. Our words are a great indicator of our Christian life. They show the condition of our hearts. If we're living for Jesus, with our lives dependent on his love and grace, our words will be full of love and grace. Our words reflect the state of our spiritual health.[7]

And so, if we have a living faith, with God's love shaping who we are, our words online will generally be positive and encouraging to others. His love flows out of us to those around us. If we speak words of anger, they will have good justification and be used to call out what is wrong, not to hurt.

If our words don't follow this pattern, that's an indicator that something deeper needs to be fixed. It isn't enough to try and improve our speech on our own. We must return to the reason why we should speak words of love and encouragement: because we've been given undeserved love and grace by the God who did everything for us at the cross.

Throughout the New Testament, we're given examples of how to use our words to build up other believers. While our words have huge power to destroy, they also have significant power to bless others. In Hebrews 10:24–25, we read:

---

7 For more on this theme, have a look at Matthew 12:33–37. Our words say a lot about the condition of our hearts.

> *And let us consider how we may spur one another on towards love and good deeds, not giving up meeting together, as some are in the habit of doing, but encouraging one another – and all the more as you see the Day approaching.*

It's a call to spend time together, encouraging one another and pushing each other on towards Jesus-centred living. We can be encouraged by fellow believers around us, and also encourage those believers we know. That includes meeting physically together when we can, but it could also include encouraging one another online.

Similarly, Romans 1:11–12 says:

> *I long to see you so that I may impart to you some spiritual gift to make you strong – that is, that you and I may be mutually encouraged by each other's faith.*

Paul, the author of the letter to the Romans, wanted to be with the believers in Rome so that he could build them up with his words. He wanted both to encourage them by his faith and be encouraged by seeing theirs too. Christians who are together, living alongside and building one another up with their words, can have huge power. We can grow much stronger when we're together and encouraging one another.

In another of Paul's letters, this time to the Thessalonian church, he reminds them, 'Therefore encourage one another and build each other up, just as in fact you are doing' (1 Thes. 5:11). This church was going from strength to strength, learning to depend on God even in very difficult circumstances. Their work of encouraging and building one another up was part of what made the church so strong. Paul always taught the believers in churches he set up to speak 'words of encouragement' (Acts 20:2), to spur one another along in their faith.

It's really hard to be a solo Christian because that's not how God designed us to be. He created us to grow together (as we'll see in chapter five on community), largely because we can use our words for mutual encouragement. That doesn't necessarily mean telling other Christians that they're wonderful all the time, but it might mean reminding them of how faithful God is to his people when they feel alone. It might mean reminding them of how generous God is to them when they get a promotion at work or some great exam results. It might mean telling them about a great example from the Bible of how good God is when they're going through something tough that makes them doubt him.

Both in our churches and online with other believers, we can encourage each another to stand firm in the faith and to live lives that serve God. We can come alongside one another when life gets tough. One of the greatest ways to help other Christians we know is to build them up in their faith with powerful words of encouragement.

As well as being encouraging to other Christians, our words are important to those outside the church. Paul tells us that our words can be a good example to those who don't yet believe in God. Paul calls on the Christians in Thessalonica to 'live lives worthy of God, who calls you into his kingdom and glory' (1 Thes. 2:12). The way that those Christians lived was important. They needed to live lives that honoured the God who had saved them, partly because of how their words and actions would be seen by those who didn't yet believe.

Likewise, when you're commenting on someone's photo, video or post, what you say tells everyone a lot about who you are. If you dive in with something negative and hurtful, people make quick judgements about your character.

Later in the same letter, Paul says:

> *Now about your love for one another we do not need to write to you, for you yourselves have been taught by God to love each other. And in fact, you do love all of God's family throughout Macedonia. Yet we urge you, brothers and sisters, to do so more and more, and to make it your ambition to lead a quiet life: you should mind your own business and work with your hands, just as we told you, so that your daily life may win the respect of outsiders and so that you will not be dependent on anybody (1 Thes. 4:9–12).*

Paul urges them to love others, to be good neighbours, to win the respect of those around them. The way they act would say something about the gospel.

Imagine you go to a café and want to order a freshly made smoothie. All the pictures on the menu look great and it's just the drink that you fancy. Then imagine that when you go up to order, the barista coughs constantly, there are flies sitting on all of the food on the counter and there's a weird smell in the air. Would you still feel excited about that smoothie or a bit nervous of what it might be like?

When we share the gospel with others, people will look at what we say and how we act. If our words are hurtful, it doesn't look like Jesus has made much of a difference to our lives! This will make it harder to share the gospel. Whereas if our words are encouraging, loving and seeking to build others up, people will be more open and responsive when we want to tell them about Jesus.

We're instructed to 'be wise in the way [we] act towards outsiders', to 'make the most of every opportunity' (Col. 4:5). The way we act towards people, especially how we use our words, says something really significant, not only about who we are but also about God.

Our words have huge power. At their worst, they can be destructive and toxic. But at their best, they can encourage other Christians and show those who don't know God why believing in him is so transformative.

THE DANGER

The tongue's destructive power

We can all remember times when our words haven't been helpful, but social media can exaggerate the destructive power of the tongue. It can be even easier to use destructive words online when we don't see the immediate reaction to what we've said or hear the words we've used out loud. Our online comments are broadcast more widely than most face-to-face conversations. Online, we also often see more extreme opinions and just can't resist reacting to them. As we can win a debate and then walk away easily, the mic-drop moment can be much more tempting.

As Christians, we need to recognise this danger. We must look at our own speech because churches that fight, bicker and complain are unhealthy. Since none of us are perfect, we know that churches will continue to have problems on this earth until Jesus comes again. In the meantime, though, we're told to recognise the destructive power of the tongue and try to stop the damage we're causing.

Perhaps there are a number of quiet Christians in your church who would be the last to complain to your minister, but online they're quick to moan about how long the sermon was or how difficult someone is to work with. Maybe you're one of those people who tries to be encouraging to others, but when you've had a hard day, it can be so tempting to gossip and complain in messages to your closest friend at church about your frustrations.

It's important that we turn away from our bickering, our gossiping and our complaining. If you've fallen into that behaviour online, admit so to God, tell him you're sorry and work to leave that all behind you. We need to stop the behind-the-back comments about other Christians and see them as they truly are: fellow brothers and sisters in Christ, saved by God, just as we have been. As part of God's church, we can use the power of words to build others up and not tear them down.

We've also seen that using unhelpful and hurtful words sets a poor example to those who don't yet trust in Jesus. If someone knows you're a Christian but sees you swearing on every online platform you use, spouting hateful views or even passively ignoring others when they reach out for help online, it's a really poor witness to what God is doing in your life.

To return to the theme of reputation we explored in chapter two, if your words are always about making yourself good, showing how proud you are of your own achievements, it passes up an opportunity to show others why Jesus tells us to be humble.

Social media gives a window into our lives that unbelievers can peer through. It's important to use our speech carefully so that we glorify God rather than rebel against him.

Our words can be dangerous and we must be careful when we speak. We should encourage other Christians and not harm what we say to unbelievers with unhelpful speech.

THE GOAL

Words of encouragement

We've identified that the goal of our speech should be to both build up fellow believers and witness to (that is, share the gospel with) others in the world.

Most churches have a small-group system, encouraging Christians not only to come along on a Sunday but also to grow relationships with other Christians in the local church during the week. In the small group I lead, it's a privilege when we get to share prayer requests with one another. We can speak wisdom into situations and comfort anyone who is struggling, encouraging them to pull close to God even when things are hard.

While those words never take the place of God's Word, the Bible, there are times in our lives when we need to hear the voices of other believers too. They can remind us of truths about God, show us examples of God at work when we can't see them and build us up when we're tempted to give up our faith.

The question we're left with is: how do we build one another up online? Maybe there are opportunities to send encouraging messages to other Christians when we know they're going through a tough time. Maybe we can create content for YouTube or TikTok that would spur other Christians on when they're struggling. Maybe we can regularly post about encouraging things that we've read in the Bible so that there's something Jesus-centred on the platforms that our Christian friends use.

Our words also act as a significant witness to those who aren't Christians. When you act differently to those who don't have a faith, trying to live like Jesus in your use of words, others notice that there is something refreshing and positive about you. Engaging positively or refusing to engage negatively because of your faith can set you apart.

Where might there be opportunities to set an example online? Maybe you could reach out with a direct message to those who are struggling, for example to a friend who always seems to post about their isolation and loneliness. Maybe you could post something positive about someone who has been through a hard time or tag them in something encouraging. Maybe you could comment helpfully on a friend's post that's getting some hurtful comments, or check in with them privately to make sure that they're okay.

As the author John Lennox says, 'No one will be interested in what we say unless they can see that our lives back up what we profess to believe.'[8]

---

8 John C. Lennox, *Have No Fear* (10Publishing, 2018), p. 39.

QUESTIONS TO THINK ABOUT

1. Where do you struggle to keep your speech helpful? Are you tempted to gossip, complain or unfairly criticise others?
2. How might your online platforms and social media look if you used them to build up and encourage other Christians?
3. How might your online platforms and social media look if you used them to set an example and tell others about Jesus?
4. What is one step this week that you could take towards building others up and sharing the gospel with your words online?

BODY

RECOGNISING OUR LIMITS

Maybe you looked at the title of this chapter and thought that we'd be talking about the use of the body on visual platforms like TikTok and Instagram. You expected to be told to keep what you post appropriate! While that's always a good idea, that's not our focus here.

In comparison to anything we do in person, our time online has one significant difference: we're not as limited by our bodies. We don't have to travel to see each person individually, so we can connect with people much further away, speaking to them over video call rather than jumping on a plane. We can have multiple conversations at once. Big news stories like engagements and pregnancy announcements travel much faster online than by telling everyone in person.

On our online platforms, we're disembodied, partially separated from the limits of our physical reality. This gives us a wider reach than ever before. While we do use our physical bodies to engage with social media, we can be free of many of our physical limits.

We can also craft our online reality to fit our desires. We can live in a world that completely revolves around us. We construct it, choosing who is in it, what they see of us, what we see of them and how we want to engage with others. Life is easier and more pleasurable, we think, when we set the rules and, to an extent, control what happens.

Tim Chester's book *Will You Be My Facebook Friend?* discusses the impact of social media. He writes, 'If you are challenged or relationships become costly, you can just scuttle off to new relationships.'[9] We can choose the people we want to connect with and quietly remove those

---

9 Tim Chester, *Will You Be My Facebook Friend?* (10Publishing, 2013), p. 34.

we don't. We can choose to stick with our current friendship groups or move on, dictating the online community we engage with down to even the fine details of how often we see a specific person's posts. Suddenly we have far more control than we could ever manage in the physical world.

And so, the move online gives us opportunities to do things we could never do before. We can rejoice in those things when they help us to glorify God. But the question remains: how can we use our physical and online presence together to glorify God? We need to work out what is good about our new online world and what we should approach with more caution. We don't want to get so attached to connecting with large numbers of people on social media that we forget the goodness of deep relationships in the physical world. However, we should try to seize opportunities to use our expanded online reach to live out our faith.

BIBLICAL PRINCIPLES

God is very different to us. His characteristics include being omniscient (knowing everything) and omnipresent (being everywhere).

Psalm 139 unpacks some of those qualities. It begins,

You have searched me, Lord,
and you know me.
You know when I sit and when I rise;
you perceive my thoughts from afar.
You discern my going out and my lying down;
you are familiar with all my ways.
Before a word is on my tongue
you, Lord, know it completely.
(vv. 1–4)

God knows us completely. He knows all that we've done, said and thought. He understands us to our very core.

As humans, we're restricted by our bodies, only knowing what we perceive through our senses. God doesn't have those limits. He is omniscient, knowing everything about us.

The psalm continues,

Where can I go from your Spirit?
Where can I flee from your presence?
If I go up to the heavens, you are there;
if I make my bed in the depths, you are there.

If I rise on the wings of the dawn,
if I settle on the far side of the sea,
even there your hand will guide me,
your right hand will hold me fast.
(vv. 7–10)

God is everywhere. We don't have to go to a special place like church to meet with him. While meeting together with other believers is good, God is no more present in a fancy, old religious building than he is in your home or school. Nor can we escape his presence.

As humans, we're restricted to our bodies, only being able to be in one place at one time. God doesn't have those limits. He is omnipresent, existing everywhere.

So, God is very different to us because he isn't confined to a human body and a human understanding. As humans, we're not like this. We're made as embodied creatures.

However, God created us with this embodied nature and declared it to be very good (Gen. 1:31). As God formed humanity from the dust, he made our bodies to be special and important. Genesis 1:26–27 records God's plan for men and women:

> *Then God said, 'Let us make mankind in our image, in our likeness, so that they may rule over the fish in the sea and the birds in the sky, over the livestock and all the wild animals, and over all the creatures that move along the ground.'*
>
> *So God created mankind in his own image,*
> *in the image of God he created them;*
> *male and female he created them.*

As we're created in the image of God, we're made to be similar to him. That doesn't mean that each of us is the same as God or is a part of God, but that each of us has characteristics that point to our Creator. We love because God is love; we seek justice because God is justice; we seek mercy because God is merciful.

While we aren't omnipresent or omniscient like God, we're created with bodies that point to him. It's a bit like when you have a physical resemblance to your parents or grandparents – maybe similar eyes or a similar height. We have characteristics that are similar to God's. There's enough resemblance for us to see clearly that we're God's creation, made in his image, even if we're sinful whereas God is perfect.

The internet promises that we can know everything, have relationships with everyone and generally be happier with the fewer limits it gives us. And yet I think we all know that isn't true. We're not created to know everything and everyone. That's too big a task! It takes us away from enjoying the people and the things we do know. The limits our bodies and minds give us aren't an accident.

God made us in his image, but in physical bodies with some limitations, because it was good to do so. It wasn't because we're really just spiritual creatures trapped in a body. Psalm 131:1–2 gives us a flavour of the goodness of our limitations:

My heart is not proud, Lord,
my eyes are not haughty;
I do not concern myself with great matters
or things too wonderful for me.
But I have calmed and quietened myself,
I am like a weaned child with its mother;
like a weaned child I am content.

We must acknowledge that God knows best. We desire the security that comes from knowing more information. We desire the popularity we feel when we know more people. But David, the writer of this psalm, knows that a constant struggle for more isn't good for us. Instead, like a weaned child with its mother, we're to cling to God for what we know about the world. Rather than seeking to know everything and everyone, our desire should be to know God better, to put our hope in him (Psalm 131:3).

To return to Psalm 139, it also says,

> *For you created my inmost being;*
> *you knit me together in my mother's womb.*
> *I praise you because I am fearfully and*
> *wonderfully made;*
> *your works are wonderful,*
> *I know that full well.*
> *(vv. 13–14)*

Once again, we're not created in bodies by accident. God created us as embodied beings. He has 'knit [us] together' in the womb, being intimately involved in our lives even before we knew it. We're commanded to praise him because of the wonderful things he has done, especially for the gracious act of creating each one of us. Therefore, we shouldn't look to our online life to escape the limits of our bodies – they're made for our good!

So, we're designed to have bodies made in the image of God. But there's more to understand than that. Our bodies also have an importance because of two things that change when we decide to follow Jesus.

In one of Paul's letters to the early church, he writes:

> *Do you not know that your bodies are temples of the Holy Spirit, who is in you, whom you have received from God? You are not your own; you were bought at a price. Therefore honour God with your bodies (1 Cor. 6:19–20).*

Firstly, when God redeemed us through Jesus, he paid the price of everything we have done wrong. Christ went through the agony of being cut off from his Father and was punished for the sins of others so that we could be forgiven. That was the price of our salvation: the Son of God dying for us. In other words, our bodies were paid for by Jesus' sacrifice because God places a value on them. That means we must honour God with our bodies.

Secondly, as followers of Jesus, our bodies are now 'temples of the Holy Spirit'. You've probably heard in sermons and teaching that God's Spirit is with you but might not talk much about what that looks like. Well, Paul tells us that the Holy Spirit lives in us; he's given to us by God. When we feel close to God and feel him guiding us, that's because his Spirit lives in us. Even when we feel far away from him, remember that he's never left us, never abandoned us, because his Spirit is inside us.

As Christians, our bodies are bought by Jesus' sacrifice and we have God's Spirit living in us. It's therefore a serious thing to misuse our bodies because they have huge value. That's one of the main reasons we want to avoid sin in our lives.

Jesus is our ultimate example of how to be an embodied creature while staying clear of sin. At his incarnation, when Jesus came to this earth as both God and man, he was perfectly sinless. Throughout his life, Jesus remained perfectly sinless. In John 1:14, we read:

> *The Word became flesh and made his dwelling among us. We have seen his glory, the glory of the one and only Son, who came from the Father, full of grace and truth.*

Jesus came to this earth in a physical body. Jesus was resurrected in a physical body. Jesus ascended to heaven in a physical body. Clearly, our bodies aren't something to avoid! Our Saviour was both perfectly God and perfectly human, appearing and accomplishing God's plan for us in the flesh.

We might expect that, because he's fully God, Jesus didn't experience the same things we do. Surely, he couldn't be tempted in the same ways we are? Surely, he didn't go through the same difficulties that we do as humans? The truth is that Jesus was also completely human and therefore went through all that we do:

> *For we do not have a high priest who is unable to feel sympathy for our weaknesses, but we have one who has been tempted in every way, just as we are – yet he did not sin (Heb. 4:15).*

Jesus, our high priest, the one who makes it possible for us to be with God, was tempted just like us. Jesus feels sympathy for our weaknesses because he experienced them, just like us. God knows what it's like to be human because he has done it himself, in the person of Jesus.

And yet, Jesus didn't sin. In all the temptation and weakness, he didn't give in. He didn't cave in. He didn't give up. Jesus lived the life we should live. He did nothing sinful and said nothing sinful (1 Pet. 2:22). His body was sinless, unstained and unblemished because he lived for God with his body. He used what God had given him to glorify his Father.

The gospel doesn't teach us to become only concerned with the soul and spiritual realms. As we're created physically, it's important that we see the importance of our bodies.

While we can use the online world as a way to reach people and connect with others, we shouldn't do this as a way to escape our physical limitations as if our bodies aren't good enough. Our bodies are made in the image of God and are inherently good and valued creations (even if broken and sinful). Let's explore the possibilities online platforms give us to do more than we could ever do before, but also acknowledge the danger that comes from becoming disconnected from our God-given bodies by trying to do too much.

THE DANGER

Consuming rather than interacting

While we can rejoice that there are more opportunities online to reach others with the gospel, we must be cautious that we don't use online platforms unhelpfully.

With fewer in-person interactions and more connections online through social media, we can get addicted to consuming information rather than interacting. Websites like Instagram and Facebook offer 'intimacy without responsibility',[10] letting us see into other people's lives while reducing the closeness of our involvement. Online we can say things about and to people that we might not in person because social media doesn't have the same immediacy and intensity.

As we saw in the psalms, we're created primarily to enjoy God, focus on him, trust him and let him transform our lives. Having him at the centre of our lives should change every

---

10 Tim Chester, *Will You Be My Facebook Friend?*, p. 34.

interaction we have with others, whether online or in the physical world.

And yet, if you looked at your own use of social media, I suspect that much of that time wouldn't be active and engaged like commenting on posts and messaging others. Most of that time would be spent passively scrolling through and absorbing content rather than being actively involved. We can be endlessly looking for more information and more people to meet.

Over time, and without a conscious challenge, we begin to expect that shallow relationships with larger numbers of people is our goal. Our desire for deep, personal relationships can begin to decrease in favour of more virtual friends, more photos and more content. Where our support networks might previously have been with a small number of people, perhaps now we tend to look to larger networks but are less likely to have deep relationships with these people.

This especially becomes a problem if we start to subconsciously expect that sort of shallow relationship with God. We can pull away from desiring a deep relationship with him because we grow used to developing larger numbers of shallower relationships. As we move further online, we're less limited in the number of 'relationships' we can form. It can be easy to drift towards that being our norm.

The answer to this isn't necessarily adding rules. We might not need to set ourselves strict time limits for our use of social media sites or numerical limits for how many friends we have online, although guidelines might be helpful for some. The answer is more likely to be regularly reflecting on our heart's motivations. Right at the start of this book, we talked about how the problem is our heart.

Rather than just setting yourself limits on the time you spend online, why not reflect regularly on your own relationship with God? Are you tending towards a shallow relationship with him or investing in a deep relationship? Does your attitude towards online friendships influence that trend?

When we spend time on social media, we must guard our hearts against a desire to always need to know more, do more, consume more and be distracted by more. Psalm 131 tells us that this isn't a good way to live.

Above all, we mustn't let ourselves get pulled away from a desire to develop a deep, vertical relationship with God. This is important when the online world promotes the opposite mindset: numerous shallow horizontal relationships.

Our relationship with God must always come first. We're made for a deep relationship with our Creator, but it can be easy to forget that online. We must also continue to invest in good relationships with others, both online and in person, if we're to use both to glorify God. So, how do we do that well?

THE GOAL

Mixed-mode mission

When we read many of the letters in the New Testament, we see how much their writers desired to see other believers in person. While the letters helped them to keep in touch, their real desire was to be together.[11] That is the way that the New Testament tends to talk about discipleship and spurring one another on in our faith. By being together, we can imitate others in how they live as a Christian. We grow as we learn together and spend time

11 For some examples of this in Paul's letters, have a look at Romans 1:8–10; 15:23–24; 1 Thessalonians 3:6; 2 Timothy 1:4.

together. The physicality of the body is good for this!

And yet, while we're embodied creatures and must acknowledge our limitations, we can appreciate developments that allow us to do more for God's glory. We never want to walk away from the goodness of our embodied nature, but our online presence allows us to supplement that. We can use social media in a similar way to these letters to the early churches, encouraging other believers and sharing the gospel when being together isn't easy.

For me, having Instagram means I can see all the baby photos from my family in the USA only moments after they're taken. I can video call my best friend living in Scotland without having to leave the sofa. I can go along to a conference on the other side of the world by joining on Zoom.

But more importantly, the online world gives us so many more opportunities to glorify God. We're able to support missionaries who are sharing the gospel far away, without having to wait for letter updates in the post. We can hear what's going on in their church by WhatsApp, see pictures on Instagram of projects they're working on or send financial gifts through a crowdfunding website when a specific need arises.

We're able to encourage Christians who we don't see much anymore, keeping in touch with friends from previous churches. We know what to pray for when we see their latest photos and videos, and they can pray similarly for us.

Having more freedom and reach online also gives us the possibility of mixed-mode mission: we can tell people about Jesus both in face-to-face conversation and online. Friends that we know online but don't get the chance to see in person regularly can now follow our lives. We need to make the most of that opportunity by showing why our faith is so important.

In all of history, it has never been this easy for believers in Jesus to share something of their faith with so many people and so easily. We have an amazing opportunity to reach out when we're with people physically and over the internet. We can make the most of mixed-mode mission to share the gospel.

Maybe you could schedule in your diary to always post on Sunday something that encouraged you at church. Maybe you could share the TikTok teaser video your church created about their new online Christianity Explored course, tagging a friend and asking them if they would like to come along with you. The glimpses people get into our lives online can be used to glorify God, so we must make sure that our online presence and wider reach show something of our faith. Let's pray that both our physical and online interactions with people show something of how great God is!

QUESTIONS TO THINK ABOUT

1. With the additional relationships and connections online platforms give you, do you feel empowered or overwhelmed?
2. Where are you tempted to become addicted to social media? How might you sustainably limit yourself?
3. How might you make the most of the increased reach you have online to tell people about Jesus?

4. How might you make the most of the increased reach you have online to support other Christians?
5. What is one step you could take this week to invest in a deep relationship with God?

COMMUNITY

SEARCHING FOR SUPPORT

How many people are you connected with online? Maybe they follow you on Instagram, are friends with you on Facebook or regularly send you snaps on Snapchat.

And how well do you know those people? Maybe they come from your school, your family, your workplace, your sports team or your craft group. Or maybe you only know them online.

Most of us are part of a huge number of communities. I'm connected with my family, old friends from school, colleagues at work, members at my current and past churches, people I've met at conferences, boyfriends and girlfriends of close friends, and even someone who taught me how to do CPR a few years ago!

The communities you're part of tell us a lot about who you are. Your school or college tells us something about you. The friends you have tell us something else. The family you're from tells us something more.

All of those communities also give us a sense of identity and belonging. They can even feel like they become part of who we are. Communities can be life-giving when they go well, but painful when relationships are difficult or come to an end.

Maybe you've changed schools and felt sadness at having to leave close friends behind. Maybe you've moved home to a new place and had to leave your football team or tennis club. Maybe you've broken up with a girlfriend or boyfriend and now don't see the same friendship group anymore because of the awkwardness of being in the same room!

Even with all the options available to us online for connecting with one another, we can still feel distant from others. Hannah Dengate and Liz Edge, in their recent book about building resilience, comment, 'Young people in the twenty-first century yearn to be connected but are feeling isolated and lonely, despite platforms being available for connection.'[12] Community is hugely important for our identity. We want to feel known, to feel loved, to have a sense of belonging.

God has created us to be community-minded people, desiring to be together because it helps us to grow. As I've previously mentioned, we're not meant to be solo Christians because we need to be part of the amazing community of church, praying for and encouraging each other.

The Bible tells us that we desire community because we're created 'by a God who himself in very nature loves connection'.[13] He is one God but three persons: Father, Son and Spirit. God's trinitarian nature models the community for which we're searching. Without being together with our church family, we're missing something of the great plan God has for us. And the good news is that our online relationships can be part

---

12 Hannah Dengate and Liz Edge, *Building Resilience in Young People* (Grove Books Limited, 2021), p. 18.

13 Hannah Dengate and Liz Edge, *Building Resilience in Young People*, p. 17.

of that expression of connection. We just need to avoid them developing in an unhealthy way.

BIBLICAL PRINCIPLES

Community isn't just a good thing. It's also a way we can experience something of what God is like.

As Christians believe that God is triune, that means we believe both these truths:

- **God is one being**: we don't worship three different Gods.
- **God is three persons**: even though they are the same God, they are three distinct persons – Father, Son and Spirit.

Michael Reeves expresses it like this: 'The Father, Son and Spirit, while distinct persons, are absolutely inseparable from each other. Not confused, but undividable. They are who they are *together*.'[14]

We have one God but we can know three distinct persons, each of whom is equally God.

Did you get that? Maybe read it again. This relationship is complex and something that I'm

14 Michael Reeves, *The Good God* (Paternoster, 2012), p. 16.

looking forward to truly understanding when I'm in eternity with God! Until then, we just have to be happy with knowing that it's a beautifully complex relationship allowing God to be both one and three.

Without getting into a deep discussion about how this works, we should notice the interconnected nature of God. We don't have a God who is isolated and alone, needing relationships with others in order to avoid loneliness. Neither do we have a God who is separate and divided, with the different parts of God fighting to be the one in control. We have a God who is diverse and different to the core, yet perfectly united.

And this tells us something about why God created humans. In his powerful book *Enjoying God*, Tim Chester tells us:

> *God didn't create the world because he needed love or wanted cheering up. He's the triune God, who lives eternally in a community of love and mutual delight. Father, Son and Spirit have all the joy they could ever want and in a far richer, purer form than we could ever provide. So why did God create the world*

> *when he didn't have to? The answer is grace – uncontrolled, unmerited grace.*[15]

God wants us to share in the communal joy he has in the Trinity. He doesn't need us in order to be joyful, but wants us to experience some of the community he enjoys in himself.

Our communities aren't the same as the Trinity and so we have to be careful how similar we see them, otherwise we could start to idolise them. However, we should notice that our communities, especially the church, aren't just good things. At their best, they're glimpses of the relationships we see within the Trinity – the relationships God has in himself.

And, as Tim Chester also points out, 'The Christian community is the main context where you experience divine joy.'[16] God wants a relationship with us. The relationships we then have with others, especially in the church, flow out from our connection with our relational God.

The church is where we learn to value both unity and diversity, a little like how God is united

---

15 Tim Chester, *Enjoying God* (The Good Book Company, 2018), p. 32.

16 Tim Chester, *Enjoying God*, p. 143.

and diverse. In our communities, we value our individual diversity but also remain united with one purpose: to become followers of Jesus who make more followers of Jesus.

Throughout the Bible, we see different communities developing. God shows us, usually through the words of his prophets and followers, which are healthy and which aren't. We therefore see principles to follow when building communities today.

To return to an example from an earlier chapter, the community at Babel was a community that fractured when they built around sin. The community wanted to be built on their own merits, to make a name for themselves (Gen. 11:4). They also wanted to avoid spreading and expanding across the earth, ignoring the command God had given them to populate the earth (Gen. 9:7). They wanted to go against God's design for community and go their own way.

God stepped in and stopped their disobedience. He caused confusion by giving them different languages so that their project of building a tower couldn't be completed. Only after his intervention were they scattered across the earth as God had commanded (Gen. 11:9). The story of the people at Babel tells us something important: communities that reject God's plan for them and rebel against his rule will not flourish.

We have no detail about individuals in this story, but can assume that being part of this community would have damaged people's view of God. Their community thought that there was no need for him because they could build a name for themselves. Their community believed that they could do all they needed without him. That would be a terrible influence on anyone trying to live for God and honour him in how they live.

As it's clear this is not how we should build our communities, we need to be aware of the influence our online communities can have on us. God needs to be integral to everything we do, whether it's our involvement in the church or our lives in the secular world. He promises in John 12:32 that he will draw all people to himself, so we're foolish to push against God's purposes. But if we spend all of our time in communities that rebel against God and ignore him, we can be tempted to do the same ourselves.

In the New Testament, there are also examples of communities going astray. Paul wrote numerous letters to the churches he'd set up. Many were to encourage those Christians to keep going, but some were written as warnings to call communities back to the true gospel of Jesus.

Paul's first letter to the Corinthian church was one of these warning letters. He identified the problems that were emerging and encouraged the church community to return to what they knew of the gospel. Unlike the people at Babel, who completely rejected God's rule, it seems that the Corinthian believers did trust in God, but they were going astray on some key issues.

These weren't small mistakes that the church was slipping into. The church had begun tolerating incest (1 Cor. 5:1–13), suing each other (1 Cor. 6:1–11), making communion a meal for the rich (1 Cor. 11:17–34) and prioritising certain spiritual gifts above others (1 Cor. 12:1 – 14:40).

They were failing to live differently as Christians. They were starting to look more like the unbelieving culture around them. So they needed to repent, say sorry for their sins and turn back towards God as their Saviour.

A healthy church community should be an expression of the relationships we see in the Trinity, being united in our purpose and valuing our differences. Instead, the Corinthian church was indulging in sin and wickedness, fighting among themselves and failing to value all of the individuals in their community.

Although the Corinthian believers professed faith in Jesus as Saviour, they needed to make drastic changes to their community if they were to glorify God in what they did. Paul reminded them that they were no longer sinners: 'But you were washed, you were sanctified, you were justified in the name of the Lord Jesus Christ and by the Spirit of our God' (1 Cor. 6:11).

The Corinthians were saved Christians, but they needed to turn away from their mistakes. They needed to live as people with a new identity. That was the purpose of Paul's first letter to the Corinthians: to show them that a good, biblical community challenges and turns away from sin.

This letter of warning was in sharp contrast to Paul's letters of encouragement. In those, he rejoiced in the work God was doing in particular church communities. One stand-out example that Paul celebrated was the Thessalonian church.

The start of that church had been difficult, to say the least, with Paul only able to stay with them for about three weeks (Acts 17:1–9). And yet, their love for the Lord was growing and God was clearly at work in their community. So Paul wrote, in his first letter to them:

> *We always thank God for all of you and continually mention you in our prayers. We remember before our God and Father your work produced by faith, your labour prompted by love, and your endurance inspired by hope in our Lord Jesus Christ ... And so you became a model to all the believers in Macedonia and Achaia. The Lord's message rang out from you not only in Macedonia and Achaia – your faith in God has become known everywhere (1 Thes. 1:2–3, 7–8).*

Their community was truly alive by God's Spirit! Their faith was causing them to do things out of love for one another and their endurance was inspired by the work of Jesus. They were being brought together by the gospel. They were an example for other Christians around them because their words and actions pointed to the message of God's amazing grace. Their faith was known all around.

I don't know about you, but that's the sort of church I want us to be! Wouldn't it be wonderful if we were known for the good things we do because of how great God is? Wouldn't it be awesome to see God so clearly at work in our community that we couldn't help but praise him for all he is doing?

We have the same God as the Thessalonian church. We have the same knowledge of what Jesus has done for us. We have the same opportunity to encourage our community to become like this. What's stopping us?!

Good relationships with one another, deep connections with one another, will flow out of a real, life-giving relationship with our living God (1 John 1:3–4). We want to grow into communities that turn from our sin, like the whole city of Nineveh did after Jonah preached God's Word to them (Jonah 3) – albeit after Jonah's brief stint in a big fish (Jonah 1)! We want to turn from our mistakes, like the Corinthian church did. We want to see God at work in our lives, as he was in the Thessalonian church.

If we do this well, it will also have an impact on the other communities we're part of. They will see something different about us as believers, marvel at the church and want to be a part of God's kingdom. A God-centred church, like the Thessalonian church, both builds up those inside and is attractive to those outside.

A church like that is the best type of community we can hope to experience this side of heaven. It's a community that comes alongside one another, that loves one another, that reflects something of who God is to the rest of the world. No church will ever do this perfectly, but we can do our best to follow that example.

James tells us more of what that might look like in practice:

> *Is anyone among you in trouble? Let them pray. Is anyone happy? Let them sing songs of praise. Is anyone among you ill? Let them call the elders of the church to pray over them and anoint them with oil in the name of the Lord. And the prayer offered in faith will make the sick person well; the Lord will raise them up. If they have sinned, they will be forgiven. Therefore confess your sins to each other and*

> *pray for each other so that you may be healed. The prayer of a righteous person is powerful and effective …*
>
> *My brothers and sisters, if one of you should wander from the truth and someone should bring that person back, remember this: whoever turns a sinner from the error of their way will save them from death and cover over a multitude of sins (James 5:13–16, 19–20).*

A good Christian community that reflects something of who God is prays together when they're in trouble. They sing songs of praise when things are going well. They confess their sins together and repent, turning away from their mistakes. They come together in prayer when someone is ill. They share gospel truths about who God is with one another when someone is wandering away from faith.

This is what a good church community looks like: it grows together and points towards the amazing God that unites us. We're bound together by our common desire to cling to the gospel and to know God more. Let's consider how we can be more like that online.

THE DANGER

Influence and isolation

There are two main dangers when dealing with online communities: negative influence and Christian isolation.

Have you ever thought about who you are connected with on your online platforms? If you didn't grow up in a church, chances are that when you first become a Christian, the majority of your online friends won't be believers. There will be hundreds of people there who need to hear about Jesus.

And yet, there is also an underlying danger that online platforms can become more unhelpful than helpful. Without a strong Christian support network online, the main voices you hear there are those of unbelievers.

We don't want to avoid or exclude our friends who aren't Christians, but we should be cautious of the influence they have on us. Given the amount of time we all spend on our phones and laptops, the views we hear are unavoidably going to influence what we think and feel. In some cases, this could be extreme, with conspiracy theories, pornography or bullying shaping what we think is normal.

In other cases, their effect can be more subtle. The more posts we see about people buying a house together and living together before marriage, the more normal it becomes to think that marriage isn't so important. The more posts we see about exam results, graduate schemes, new job promotions and awards, the more normal it becomes to think that the goal in life is to be better, earn more and prove yourself. The more we see about friends who have the 'perfect life' – getting serious with their partner, having children, becoming engaged and buying the ideal home – the more normal it becomes to think that having the perfect family, the ideal wedding and the nicest house is the ultimate goal of life.

Those things aren't all negative in themselves, but we can easily be dragged into an unbiblical worldview where we see those things as more important than our relationship with God. The narratives we hear that make no mention of God can distract us from what is important: knowing that our primary identity is as God's children.

Consider reviewing your social media connections to ensure that through them you can both encourage and be encouraged by

Christian friends. Be wise when you see the narratives of the world telling you to look outside of God for your hope and joy. Rejoice when you see someone praising God and living for him in their life.

Some Christians face the opposite problem: all of their friends and followers are Christians! We should rejoice that they will have plenty of supportive people around them who will encourage them in their faith, share lots of Christian content and demonstrate how to live as a Christian. However, it becomes a danger when we find ourselves in a Christian bubble.

We lose the possibility of fruitful evangelism online if we have no one to evangelise to! I started with an online friendship group full of those who already believe in Jesus. As a result, there weren't many people I could virtually invite to carol services or message online when I knew that they were interested in exploring faith. Living in a visibly different way online, with the purpose of showing something of God's character, needs to be seen by non-believers!

Maybe when you join a community group or sports team, or you make friends in a coffee shop who don't know Jesus yet, you could try to form an online connection too. While that doesn't mean ignoring them in person, it increases the opportunities for them to see the difference God makes in your life and opens up more opportunities for them to come to you with big questions about life and faith.

Avoid the dangers of having either a Christian bubble or an online platform with no Christian support. Find the balance where you can be encouraged in your faith and have clear chances to share the gospel with those you know.

THE GOAL

Sharing life together

Do you spend time throughout the week with those at your church, rather than just coming together for a service on a Sunday? No church is perfect, but a good one will prioritise spending time together in this way. This gives opportunities to study the Bible together, pray together, share meals together and share the gospel with outsiders together. To be a church family means being around one another! Meeting together to worship God and encourage one another should be something we really look forward to when that's physically possible. There's no substitute for spending time together. And as we saw in chapter three, we want to build one another up and encourage one another in our faith with our words. We want to be the sort of community that others want to join.

So, what does this community life look like online? It means thinking through all of the opportunities we have to live out our faith in person and considering how we can extend (not replace) that online.

More and more churches are beginning to invest in online materials and events to support their members, as it's hard when we can't be together. Paul and James would have felt the pain of not being with the churches they had planted. Both persecution and the need to spread the gospel across the world meant that they couldn't be together face to face. They had to use letters to share their lives with these churches. Today, we can do something similar online.

During the coronavirus pandemic that began in 2020, churches couldn't meet face to face and so many moved their services online. To keep our relationships with one another going, we not only went for walks with one another and shared meals by dropping food at each other's doors, but also prayed together at online meetings and spent time eating together and socialising over video calls. It was up to us as individual believers to make a difference and to work really hard at keeping our church community healthy. While we rejoice that in-person meetings have since returned, there are parts of our online communities that we should be careful not to lose.

In my church, people joined us online who would have really struggled to be with us physically, even in normal times. Continuing some of those streaming services and not leaving behind some of our online socials is important, otherwise these new support networks will fall apart. Our mid-week groups have created WhatsApp groups to keep in contact with each other for prayer requests. Our youth groups have invested in a new messaging app so that everyone can encourage one another between sessions. Our daytime ministries have found that volunteers who are at home can input more into daytime ministries by dropping in online by Zoom during their work breaks.

It's important to continue to meet in person as being together physically generally fosters community more strongly, but as Christians let's think through what we can do to encourage one another online. Maybe you could set up a prayer triplet with two of your friends, sending prayer requests each morning via a WhatsApp group but then meeting together physically once a month in a coffee shop to pray through those things. Maybe you could regularly tag your friends in something encouraging that you've seen on a Christian Instagram page and then follow it up the next time you see them at church. Maybe you could occasionally send Christian memes to each other. (One of my mid-week groups does that between meetings and it regularly makes me laugh out loud in public places, while no one else understands what is going on!)

We can also use our Christian community to share the gospel online. The Thessalonian church was known all around for the good things they were doing, which caused the gospel to ring out from their community. We shouldn't only be part of our Christian community, otherwise we won't have any relationships with non-believers. That will make sharing the gospel incredibly difficult! It's good to be part of the local football team, to spend lots of time with family and to meet with those who love the same hobby as you. The challenge is how we engage online in those communities while pointing to Jesus.

Firstly, ensure that you live differently in your other communities. Be positive and encouraging in the football team's WhatsApp group so that people are more open to you talking about Jesus after the match next week. Make your craft project personal by showing something of your faith in your design and then posting it online with an explanation of the reason behind your work.

Secondly, share what your church is doing with the communities you're involved in. Invite them to the next online Christianity Explored course. Tell them about the community BBQ the church is running by inviting the whole group on Facebook. Instead of only posting every time your netball team wins a match or you've been to a great concert, why not post to rejoice that you've met with God at church this week? Maybe you could even post on your Instagram that you'd love for people to send prayer requests to you!

And finally, make it clear online that your church comes first over your other communities.

We shouldn't ignore other communities in favour of isolating ourselves in a Christian bubble, but we should show that church is our priority in how we spend our time and where our loyalties lie.

Maybe you could start your social media bio with the fact that you're a Christian, rather than with where you go to school. Maybe when you can't commit to the rugby match on a Sunday morning, you could share something online about church that your rugby mates will see. Then they'll know that you weren't just in bed that morning, but that you chose church over playing on a Sunday.

The church community is the place where we want to spend time together and that includes being together online. We must both encourage one another and use our church community as an opportunity to share the gospel.

QUESTIONS TO THINK ABOUT

1. What are the things you want from being part of a community? Do you get them in the church?
2. What is the balance of your online community? Do you rely more heavily on Christian or non-Christian friends?
3. How does that balance affect you? Is this positive or negative?
4. What is one step you could take this week to make sure that you have both Christian and non-Christian online connections?

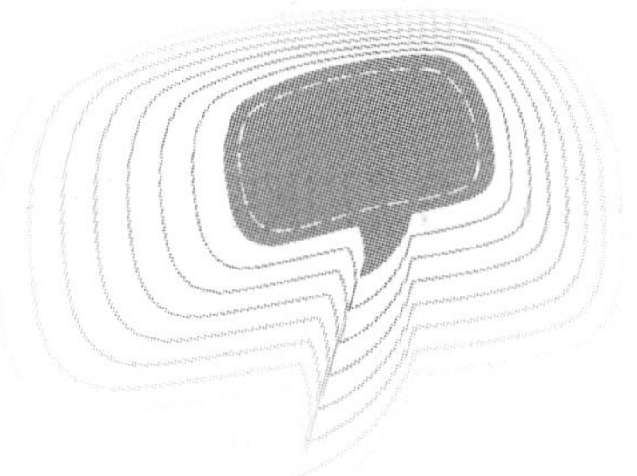

CONCLUSION

THE GOSPEL TRANSFORMS OUR ONLINE IDENTITY

My day job mostly involves working with teenagers and telling them how great God is. I encourage them to read the Bible for themselves to see the difference Jesus makes. One of the most common questions I get asked is what to do when the Bible doesn't talk about something because it didn't exist 2000 years ago.

In the past five chapters, I hope you've seen that the Bible isn't silent on the issue of our online presence, although it's not specifically mentioned. The prophets, historians and church leaders who wrote the words in the Bible did so by the inspiration of God's Spirit. While they had no idea of what was to come with the invention of the internet, the themes they unpack speak into contemporary issues.

The question for you is: how might what you've read impact the way you live?

For Martin, his goal is to remember that he is a child of God before anything else. Every time he is tempted to see himself first as a boyfriend, a dodgeball player or a part-time shopworker, he needs to cling to his God-given primary identity. His primary identity – knowing that he is loved by his heavenly Father – is too good to be second best.

For Grace, there's no longer a need to worry about making every online post show herself in the best light. She knows that God gives her a name and reputation based on her relationship with him, not her own good works. Her biggest lesson is that she needs to rely on God's name and his relationship with her rather than craving the approval she gets from others in likes and comments.

For Zoe, her questions about how she can best use her words are answered by looking at Jesus. He shows her what she can do to avoid the hurt that unhelpful words can cause. He also shows her how much good her words can do when she uses them to share the gospel and to encourage her Christian friends.

For Joe, it's important to know that he's made not only for the online world. God created him as an embodied creature, made in the image of God. He knows that he is loved because of Jesus, even if he sometimes feels broken and sinful. His challenge is to avoid becoming addicted to consuming more and more content online. Instead, he's looking to develop a deeper relationship with God and enjoying building mixed-mode friendships, sharing the gospel both online and in person.

For Ruth, getting involved in her church community feels a little bit less scary when she knows that her desire for deeper relationships with others is how God designed her to be. Making time to find new friends in the church should be a real priority, both physically and online. She also needs to make sure that she gets good time with those who don't know Jesus so that she can share what she believes.

As we close, let us rejoice in all that we have learned about who God is. God loves us, even though we're broken sinners. Jesus went to the cross and endured terrible suffering so that we can have a future with God, even though we make poor decisions and rebel against God. It isn't our actions that save us; it's God's incomparable grace.

We now live our lives for God because we want to thank him for all he has done for us and glorify him with everything we do. Pointing to God in this way doesn't just apply face to face. It applies online too.

When online, let's look to our status as God's child above all else. Let's make our online connections and our use of social media show something of our faith. Let's pray that those around us look at our online presence and see clearly that God is at work in our lives.

I would encourage you to spend time reflecting on these final questions. Try not to forget the things you've learned, leaving them on the shelf with this book! Why not spend a few days thinking about each theme and considering how your online presence can be transformed by your relationship with our gracious God?

QUESTIONS TO THINK ABOUT

1. Where in the Bible can you see something of God's plan for your life online?
2. Which of the five themes are you going to focus on first?
3. What are the danger signs in your life when your social media habits become unhelpful? How are you going to make sure you notice these? Can someone help you with this?
4. What is one step you could take this week to glorify God in your life?

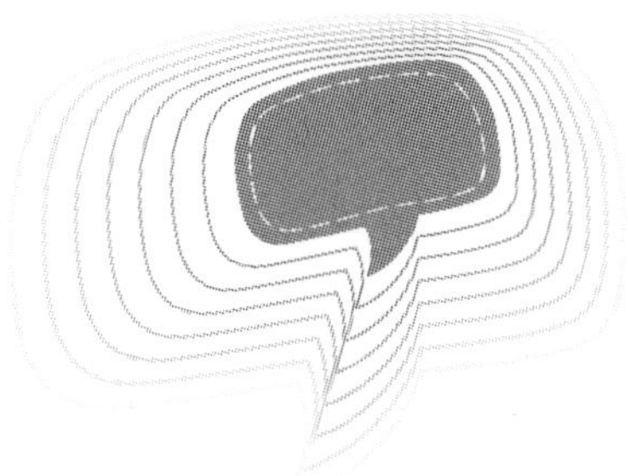

ACKNOWLEDGEMENTS

This book wouldn't have been written without the support of so many people. To Lutterworth Church and the whole Wycliffe Fellowship, thank you for supporting my work in so many ways. Without your friendship, prayer and practical support, giving me the time to minister to young people and grow in my own relationship with God, none of this would have been possible.

I've been so encouraged seeing God at work in our children and young people, and have been privileged to see so many of you grow into disciples of Jesus. Thank you for trying out some of my ideas at our Rooted Youth Group and Sunday Youth Night as I pulled this book together, and for putting up with my constant laughter! My prayer is that you would all one day call upon God as your Saviour and grow to love him with all your heart.

Thank you to all who proofread drafts and sharpened my thoughts, including Tom, Charlie, Jerry, Ben, Heather, Sarah, Nathan, Mike, Phil and Anna. Thank you to my editor, Julie, for patiently and meticulously working through my manuscript to make it the best it could be.

A particular thank you to both my parents, Andrew and Wendy, who've read so many of the things I've written over the years. They've encouraged me to be the best I can be, but I know that whatever I did, it wouldn't change their unending love for me.

And finally, many thanks to my wife, Lizzi. Thank you for reading countless drafts, listening to endless ideas and being so gracious when I'm home late after a particularly exciting youth group! Above all, thank you for sharing your life with me. May we see God at work in all that we do!

DIG INTO
MATTHEW
A DAILY BIBLE STUDY
CHRIS RANSON
GENUINE
BECOMING A
EAL TEENAGER
C.B. MARTIN
H WARREN W. WIERSBE
GAIN THE
WHOLE
WORLD?
C.B. MARTIN

10 Publishing